Arden the Airedale

──── Based on a True Story ────

Judy Mercer

Archway Publishing books may be ordered through booksellers or by contacting:

Archway Publishing
1663 Liberty Drive
Bloomington, IN 47403
www.archwaypublishing.com
1 (888) 242-5904

ISBN: 978-1-4808-7260-8 (sc)
ISBN: 978-1-4808-7261-5 (hc)
ISBN: 978-1-4808-7259-2 (e)

Print information available on the last page.

Archway Publishing rev. date: 1/16/2019

For my daughter, Alicia, whose first
real true love has four legs.
For my sons, Lee and Seth, for their
love of adventure and animals.
For my new granddaughter, Kate, and
the amazing journey to come.
For my son-in-law, Mike, for being such
a wonderful addition to the family.

Arden was a happy pup. He left his mom and went to live with a lovely young lady named Alicia.

Alicia got Arden as a Christmas present when she was a freshman in college. Alicia had a lot of friends and Arden loved being around all of them. They were always excited to see him.

Arden and Alicia had many adventures together. Arden enjoyed going to Granny's house and visiting Azar the horse, Bessie the cow, and Bindi Sue and Fluff the cats. It was fun running on the farm. The grass was soft on his paws. The air smelled fresh. The Blue Jays sang beautiful songs in the Wild Cherry trees as the squirrels jumped quickly from limb to limb. Addie and Sabrina, the other dogs there, were his best friends. Arden liked to wrestle with them, and they all liked to chase the squirrels through the woods.

Arden felt like an important part of Alicia's family. Although he did have four legs and a furry body, she gave him baths, cut his hair, and told him that he was the cutest thing ever!

One day Alicia had to take a trip to see her friend Mike. Mike lived far away in another city and Alicia couldn't take Arden with her. Alicia would try to explain to Arden that she would be back. He would cock his head sideways trying to understand and she would give him a big kiss. Arden loved this because she felt like his mom. He didn't understand her leaving him behind, because he was able to go most anywhere with her.

Alicia took Arden to a friend's house. Arden had been around this friend before. He liked her. Arden had fun playing with the little boy here and laying in the warm sunshine. A couple days went by and he started to miss Alicia.

One day the gate of the yard was left open and Arden decided he might venture out and see if he could find Alicia. He knew he probably shouldn't, but he missed her so much and maybe he could find her. "Where could she be? She has been gone too long!"

I'll just poke my head around the corner and see if I see her, thought Arden. So he did. He started walking and walking, and then he went around the next corner. The wind felt good on his curly coat as he trotted along. Pretty soon Arden could not see the house or gate anymore. He saw different houses...strange houses, and strange people!

All of a sudden Arden was in the road. It was a wide road. He was never allowed in the road without Alicia. There were cars and trucks everywhere!

Arden became overwhelmed and really scared. He started to whimper and whine. What should he do? Where was Alicia? Cars were honking, trucks were beeping. He tried to run, but he was right in the middle of a highway!

Arden froze—he just could not take another step. He felt very sad and very sick. He had never missed Alicia so much. If he could just get back to where Alicia left him, he would never ever leave the yard again!

Screech....a car came to a sudden stop!
Arden tucked his tail between his legs.
He thought the car was going to hit
him. He trembled all over his body.
"Who is this?" thought Arden.

A man stopped, quickly put Arden into his car, and drove off. Tired and sad, Arden wilted into the car seat. All Arden could think about now was if he would ever see Alicia again. The man drove on and Arden just laid there. He was too afraid to do anything else.

Soon the man came to a stop on the side of the road. Arden perked up. "Am I home?" he wondered anxiously. But he was not. The kind man put out a gentle hand to pet Arden, examined his collar, and then made a phone call.

Arden's collar had a bone-shaped metal tag with Alicia's phone number on it. The man called Alicia and told her that he had Arden. Arden could hear her voice. He quickly started to feel better! "Now I know why my collar jingled all the time", thought Arden. "It was that silly tag. Alicia must have put that tag on me in case I get lost when she is not around. She really is my mom!"

Soon Alicia's friend came and picked up Arden. Arden barked a big "thank you" to the man and licked his hand. He was so grateful to this man for rescuing him.

Arden was happy to see Alicia's friend. He knew now that he could get back to that yard where Alicia would find him.

It made Arden feel good that there was so much kindness in others. Because of this man, Arden could finally get back home.

The next day Alicia came to get Arden. Arden howled in his best "I missed you a lot" voice and licked her face. Alicia couldn't stop hugging Arden. "I missed you, too, Arden!"

JUDY MERCER and her husband, Barry, live on a farm in Kentucky. Their three children spent their childhoods growing up there.

Printed in the United States
By Bookmasters